VERTEX

INTERNATIONAL PRIVATE BRAND
DESIGN COMPETITION

EDITED BY:

CHRISTOPHER DURHAM,
PRESIDENT, MY PRIVATE BRAND

PHILLIP RUSSO,
PUBLISHER, GLOBAL RETAIL BRANDS

folio28

CHARLOTTE, NORTH CAROLINA

Volume VI: Vertex Awards International Retail Brand Design Competition

Office Depot Tul Pen image by Teri Campbell of teristudios.com

Published by Folio28 LLC, Charlotte, NC
www.folio28.com
www.mypbrand.com
ISBN 978-0-9915220-9-5
First Edition

TABLE OF CONTENTS

GOLD

SILVER

BRONZE

Every year The Vertex Awards brings us the best in private brand packaging design, and this year was no exception. With a record number of entries, from 33 countries representing the absolute best in package design from around the globe including the first ever entry from India.

This year's competition includes several exciting additions. The first is the debut of the new Vertex trophy designed by the artisans at Cristaux International. The brushed aluminum monolith with the cutout of the iconic Vertex "V" is the essence of bold modern design, making it the ultimate expression of private brand.

This year we are also dramatically enhancing and expanding the Vertex Awards and celebration. We will hold the awards ceremony, winners exhibit, and celebration at Velocity: The My Private Brand Conference on April 30, in Charlotte, NC. Then on October 22, 2019 we will continue the celebration of the Vertex winners with an exhibit and cocktail party at the Velocity Europe Conference in Lisbon, Portugal.

Also new this year we are excited to debut a new award. This will be the Vertex Retailer of the Year award. The honor will be given to the two retailers who achieve the highest overall score based on their winning entries. We have split the globe into two broad regions, and each region will have one winner. The winner from North America, Central America, and South America will receive their award at the Velocity conference in the United States. The winner from Europe, Asia, the Middle East, Oceania,

and Africa will receive their award at the Velocity Europe conference October 22, 2019, in Lisbon, Portugal.

We would like to thank our panel of judges from around the world who took their charge to heart, devoting their time and energy to selecting the best of the best: Paco Adin, Rick Barrack, Danielle Beal, Paula Bunny, Connie Cao, Chris Cheung, Charlene Codner, Steven Cox, Maria Dubuc, Michael Duffy, Guillermo Dufranc, Masanori Eto, Loe Limpens, Fred Richards, Jens Sievert, Nick Vaus and Zhou Wenjun. Thank you!

Qualifying designs for Vertex must have been introduced instore between November 2017 and November 2018. Judges scored each entry on five criteria: design, information architecture, originality, structure, and x-factor. An overall numeric score was then assigned to each entry. Gold, Silver and Bronze Awards were awarded based on the numeric score. As a result, there may be multiple winners in some categories of a given award and no winners in other categories.

The scoring system was developed to reward the best private brand package design in the world, not mediocrity. To protect the integrity of the process, judges were not allowed to vote on work by their agency. All voting was entered online, and votes were collected and tabulated independently, by VOCCII. This competition has been a labor of love. We know you will find inspiration in the winners.

Christopher Durham
Founder, My Private Brand

Phillip Russo
Publisher, Global Retail Brands

O F S

2019 VERTEX AWARDS

BEST

HOW

REAL KATZENNAHRUNG

RETAILER: Real
COUNTRY: Germany
CATEGORY: G7. Pet Products
AGENCY: Yellow Dress Retail
CREDITS:
Brand Manager: Anamaria Radoi
Art Director: Michelle Romeo-Wiegman
Designer: Lisanne Snoek
Illustrator: Willemijn de Lint

PUBLIS

SHER'S CHOICE

PUBLISHER'S CHOICE

TUL PRO PENS

RETAILER: Office Depot Office Max
COUNTRY: USA
CATEGORY: H7. Office
AGENCY: Office Depot
CREDITS:
Brand Managers: Rachel Tibor & Josie Sandoval
Creative Lead: Danielle Stella-Fischer
Design Manager: Marjolijn Elbert-Chung
Production Designer: Terry Coffy
Print Manager: Sharon Gross

Package Image by Teri Campbell of teristudios.com

PUBLISHER'S CHOICE

CO-OP
HALLOWEEN

RETAILER: CO-OP
COUNTRY: UK
CATEGORY: B4. Holiday Or Limited-Edition
AGENCY: Equator Design
CREDITS:
Brand Manager: Brooke Fletcher
Account Manager: Tony Hornby
Art director/Designer: Glyn Robinson, Stephen Reilly

This year we are excited to debut a new award. This will be the Vertex Retailer of the Year award. The honor will be given to the two retailers who achieve the highest overall score based on their winning entries. We have split the globe into two broad regions, and each region will have one winner. The winner from North America, Central America, and South America will receive their award at the Velocity conference on April 30, 2019, in the United States. The winner from Europe, Asia, the Middle East, Oceania, and Africa will receive their award at the Velocity Europe conference October 22, 2019, in Lisbon, Portugal.

RE

OF THE

TAILER

E YEAR

ALBE

RETAILER OF THE YEAR

EUROPE, ASIA, THE MIDDLE EAST, OCEANIA, AND AFRICA

RT HEIJN

This year, Ahold Delhaize owned Dutch grocer Albert Heijn received a total of four Vertex Awards. The four Gold winning entries represent the largest number of wins by any retailer in this year's contest as well as the highest cumulative score from the judging panel.

RETAILER OF THE YEAR

This year, online club retailer Boxed adds to its growing tradition of winning Vertex Awards by winning three awards as well as the highest cumulative score from the judging panel.

GO

DABIZ MUÑOZ SALSAS XO

RETAILER: El Corte Inglés
COUNTRY: Spain
CATEGORY: B3. Licensed Or Co-Brand
AGENCY: Supperstudio
CREDITS:
Creative Director: Paco Adín
Account Director: Lourdes Morillas
Account Manager: Susana Seijas
El Corte Inglés Corporate Private Brand Management: José A. Rojano

SWEE!

RETAILER: Redmart
COUNTRY: Singapore
CATEGORY: B1. New Brand
AGENCY: Anthem Worldwide, Singapore
CREDITS:
Brand Manager (Redmart): Nupur Agrawal
Creative/Strategic Direction: Spencer Ball
Design Direction: Steven Soh
Design: Simone Hui
Account Lead: Anne Kernahan, Cheryl Chia

FRESH THYME PREMIUM

RETAILER: Fresh Thyme Farmers Market
COUNTRY: USA
CATEGORY: B1. New Brand
AGENCY: The Creative Pack
CREDITS:
Creative Director: Danielle Beal
Designer: Emma Tung
Project Manager: Fern Serna

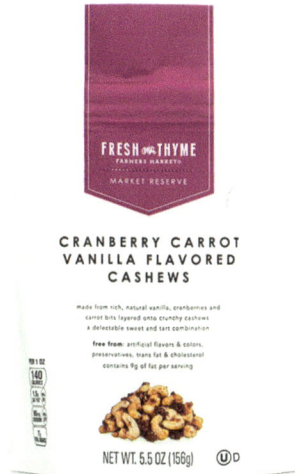

CRANBERRY CARROT
VANILLA FLAVORED
CASHEWS

Made from rich, natural vanilla, cranberries and
carrot bits layered onto crunchy cashews
a delectable sweet and tart combination

free from: artificial flavors & colors,
preservatives, trans fat & cholesterol
contains 9g of fat per serving

NET WT. 5.5 OZ (156g)

WILD BLUEBERRY
LEMON OATMEAL
GLAZED ALMONDS

made from almonds, gluten free oats and
wild blueberries with a light, zesty lemon glaze

free from: artificial flavors & colors,
preservatives, trans fat & cholesterol
contains 10g of fat per serving

NET WT. 7 OZ (198g)

ARRABBIATA
PASTA SAUCE

NET WT. 25.5 OZ (1 LB 9.5 OZ) 723g

TOMATO BASIL
PASTA SAUCE

NET WT. 25.5 OZ (1 LB 9.5 OZ) 723g

FETTUCCINE

SPAGHETTI

PENNE RIGATE

ORECCHIETTE

FUSILLONI

FRANKIE & FRIENDS

RETAILER: Woolworths
COUNTRY: Australia
CATEGORY: G7. Pet Products
AGENCY: Boxer & Co.
CREDITS:
Designer and Illustrator: Nicoletta Braach-Maksvytis
Creative Director: Mark Haygarth
Project Manager: Tessa Carr
Client Project Lead: Sophie Challenor

MADRE MIA: THE WANTED

RETAILER: Modelo Continente Hipermercados SA
COUNTRY: Portugal
CATEGORY: B1. New Brand
AGENCY: Fuel
CREDITS:
Fuel Agency
SonaeMC Packaging & Design Team

PRINCE &SPRING JACKPOT POPCORN

RETAILER: Boxed.com
COUNTRY: USA
CATEGORY: G3. Packaged Goods
AGENCY: Boxed
CREDITS:
VP Private Brands: Jeff Gamsey
Creative Director: Chris Cheung
VP Design: Ryan Carl
Senior Product Developer: Brandon Wehmeyer
Senior Package Designer: Vera Atamian
Brand Manager & Copy Writer: Annslee Deluca
Graphic Artist: Monica Kim

PRINCE & SPRING
140
CALORIES
PER BAG
JACKPOT
SWEET & SALTY
POPCORN
NET WT 1 OZ (28g)

PRINCE & SPRING
90
CALORIES
PER BAG
JACKPOT
SEA SALT
POPCORN
NET WT 0.6 OZ (17g)

WARPED ROOTS BEER

RETAILER: Hy-Vee
COUNTRY: USA
CATEGORY: G5. Beverages: Alcoholic
AGENCY: Meyocks
CREDITS:
Hy-Vee and Meyocks Package Design Team

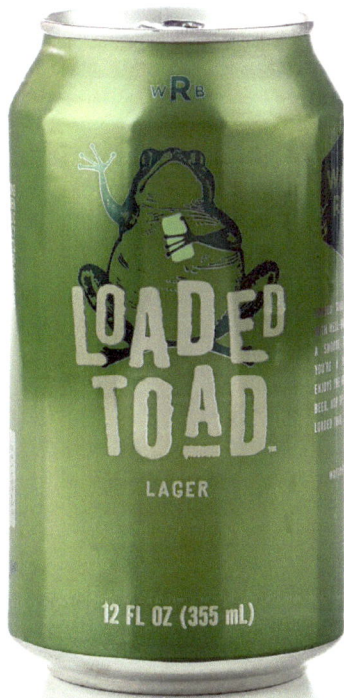
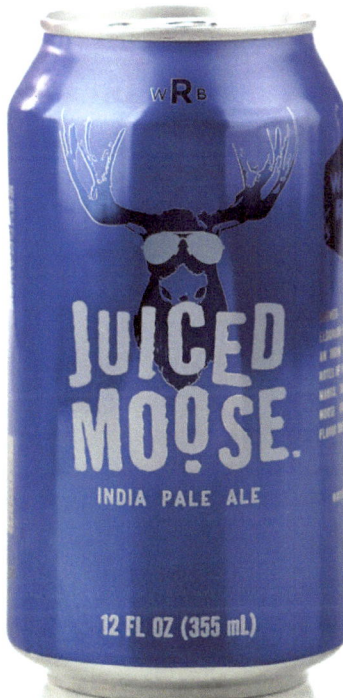
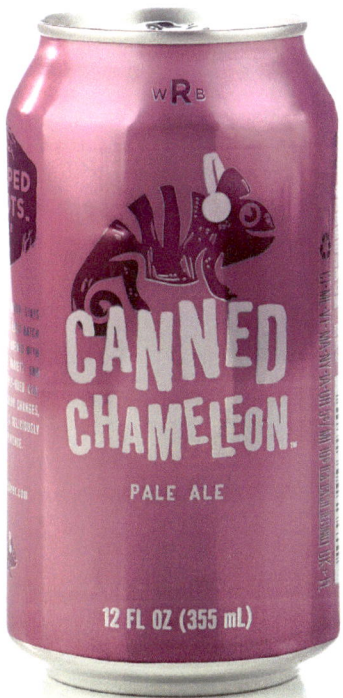

OVERJOY LIGHT ICE CREAM

RETAILER: Hy-Vee
COUNTRY: USA
CATEGORY: G4. Frozen
AGENCY: Meyocks
CREDITS:
Hy-Vee and Meyocks Package Design Team

overjoy

Mint Chip
Mint light ice cream with chocolaty chips
310 calories per pint
light ice cream
67% FEWER CALORIES AND 83% LESS FAT THAN REGULAR ICE CREAM
GOOD SOURCE OF PROTEIN
NET 1 PT (473 mL)

overjoy™

Chocolate Peanut Butter
Chocolate light ice cream with a peanut butter swirl
360 calories per pint
light ice cream
65% FEWER CALORIES AND 73% LESS FAT THAN REGULAR ICE CREAM
GOOD SOURCE OF PROTEIN
NET 1 PT (473 mL)

overjoy™

Chocolate Cookie
Chocolate light ice cream with a cookie swirl
390 calories per pint
light ice cream
55% FEWER CALORIES AND 57% LESS FAT THAN REGULAR ICE CREAM
GOOD SOURCE OF PROTEIN
NET 1 PT (473 mL)

ove

Cinnamo
Cinnamon caramel cream with cinnam
360
light ice crea
61% FEWER CALORIES AND 75% LESS FAT THAN REGULA
GOOD SOURCE OF PROTEIN
NET 1 PT (473 m

overjoy™

S'mores
Chocolate and marshmallow flavored light ice cream with chocolaty chunks and a graham cracker swirl
390 calories per pint
light ice cream
60% FEWER CALORIES AND 71% LESS FAT THAN REGULAR ICE CREAM
GOOD SOURCE OF PROTEIN
NET 1 PT (473 mL)

overjoy™

Birthday Cake
Cake flavored light ice cream with pieces and candy sprinkles
350 calories per pint
light ice cream
60% FEWER CALORIES AND 71% LESS FAT THAN REGULAR ICE CREAM
GOOD SOURCE OF PROTEIN
NET 1 PT (473 mL)

overjoy™

Sea Salt Caramel
Caramel light ice cream with a sea salt caramel swirl
310 calories per pint
light ice cream
66% FEWER CALORIES AND 82% LESS FAT THAN REGULAR ICE CREAM
GOOD SOURCE OF PROTEIN
NET 1 PT (473 mL)

EL CORTE INGLÉS MUESLI

RETAILER: El Corte Inglés

COUNTRY: Spain

CATEGORY: G3. Packaged Goods

AGENCY: Supperstudio

CREDITS:

Creative Director: Paco Adín:

Account Director: Lourdes Morillas

Account Manager: Susana Seijas

El Corte Inglés Corporate Private Label Brand Management: José A. Rojano

FRUITYLAB SHOWER GEL

RETAILER: Kontigo / Eurocash S.A.
COUNTRY: Poland
CATEGORY: P5. Body Care
AGENCY: Aleksandra Szmak Studio
CREDITS:
Creative Direction & Execution: Aleksandra Szmak
Visualization: Kontigo

SPAR COFFEE

RETAILER: SPAR Holding B.V.
COUNTRY: Netherlands
CATEGORY: B1. New Brand
AGENCY: Yellow Dress Retail
CREDITS:
Brand Manager: Jan-Hein van Spaandonk
Creative Director: Michelle Romeo-Wiegman
Designer: Nicole Moonen
Illustrator: Willemijn de Lint

CULINARIA

RETAILER: Schnucks
COUNTRY: USA
CATEGORY: B2. Redesigned Brand
AGENCY: Equator Design
CREDITS:
Creative Director: Jennifer Gaeto
Lead Designer: Josh Weigelt
Photographer: Lisamarie Cerny, Amy Stallard
Account Director: Alyssa Cioffi

CARAMEL CRAVE
Ice Cream

NET 48 FL OZ (1.5 QT) 1.42L

PREMIUM BELGIAN
**ORANGE &
ALMONDS**
Dark Chocolate

REAL PREMIUM
**FROSTED SUGAR
COOKIE**
Ice Cream

ARTISAN
**GARLIC
PARMESAN**
FLAVORED

Kettle Cooked Chips

Creamy aged parmesan cheese
with a hint of garlic

SMALL BATCH
SLOW COOKED

NO ARTIFICIAL COLORS OR FLAVORS

ARTISAN
**SPICY
JALAPEÑO**
FLAVORED

Kettle Cooked Chips

Boldly seasoned for a fresh
and fiery jalapeño kick

SMALL BATCH
SLOW COOKED

NO ARTIFICIAL COLORS OR FLAVORS

ARTISAN
**MESQUITE
BARBECUE**
FLAVORED

Kettle Cooked Chips

A distinctive blend of smoky,
sweet and tangy barbecue

SMALL BATCH
SLOW COOKED

REAL PREMIUM
**BEACH BUM
COCONUT RUM**
Ice Cream

NET 48 FL OZ (1.5 QT) 1.42L

WELLSLEY FARMS WINE

RETAILER: BJ's Wholesale Club
COUNTRY: USA
CATEGORY: G5. Beverages: Alcoholic (Liquid)
AGENCY: Marketing By Design
CREDITS:
Creative Director: David Ziegler-Voll
Designer: Kailen Eaker
Production Artist: Rob Monroe
Project Manager: Alison Hom

FRED'S CHIPS

RETAILER: Fred's Inc.
COUNTRY: USA
CATEGORY: G3. Packaged Goods
AGENCY: Marketing By Design
CREDITS:
Creative Director: David Ziegler-Voll
Designer: Katie Vinci
Production Artist: Deanna Vosburgh
Project Manager: Ashley Smits
Account Manager: Christopher Thaemert

7-SELECT ICED COOKIES

RETAILER: 7-Eleven
COUNTRY: USA
CATEGORY: G3. Packaged Goods
AGENCY: Marketing By Design
CREDITS:
Creative Director: David Ziegler-Voll
Art Director: Sandra Button
Production Artist: Roger Calado
Account Manager: Austin Sniezek

AH
CORDIALS

RETAILER: Albert Heijn
COUNTRY: Netherlands
CATEGORY: G6. Beverages: Non-Alcoholic
AGENCY: Millford
CREDITS:
Brand manager: Sophie van Felius
Art director: Tahir Idouri
Designer: Jon Sonneveld
Account director: Sascha Goutier
Studio: Charlotte van Delft

BARISSIMO PASSPORT SERIES

RETAILER: ALDI US
COUNTRY: USA
CATEGORY: G3. Packaged Goods
AGENCY: Equator Design
CREDITS:
Creative Director: Jennifer Gaeto
Lead Designer: Alysha Balog & Amy Hawker
Illustrator: Alysha Balog
Account Manager: Bridget Martin

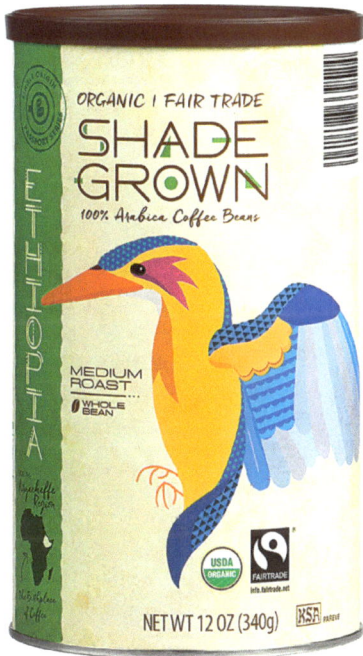

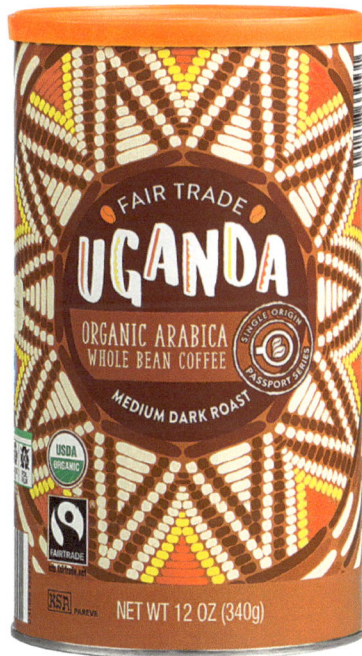

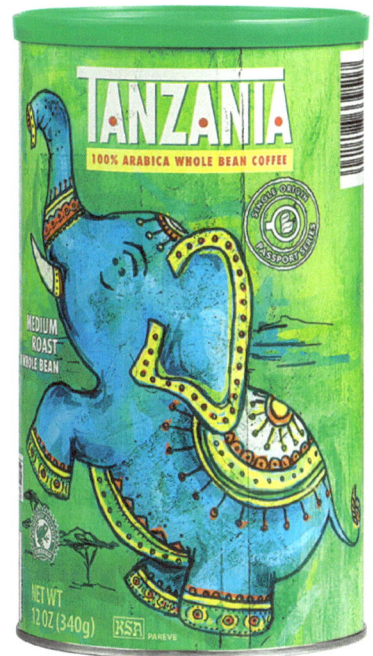

MACRO KOMBUCHA

RETAILER: Woolworths
COUNTRY: Australia
CATEGORY: G6. Beverages: Non-Alcoholic
AGENCY: Marque Brand Consultants
CREDITS:
Senior Designer: Anita Williams
Senior Account Manager: Blanca Veiga
Brand Manager: Kate Walker
Design Specialist: Jade Tonkin

AH
MORE

RETAILER: Albert Heijn
COUNTRY: The Netherlands
CATEGORY: G3. Packaged Goods
AGENCY: dBOD
CREDITS:
Brand Director/Strategist: Evelyn Hille/dBOD
Senior Design Director: Ditte Glebbeek/dBOD

Rode Linzen PENNE
100% gemaakt van Peulvruchten
Glutenvrij
6 MIN. KOKEN
van nature bron van vezels en eiwitten
Groene erwten FUSILLI
100% gemaakt van Peulvruchten
Glutenvrij
5 MIN. KOKEN
van nature bron van vezels en eiwitten
Gele Linzen LASAGNE
90% gemaakt van Peulvruchten
Glutenvrij
35-40 min. OVENTIJD
van nature bron van vezels en eiwitten
Gele Linzen SPAGHETTI
90% gemaakt van peulvruchten
Glutenvrij
8 MIN. KOKEN
van nature bron van vezels en eiwitten
Een verrijking voor jouw keuken
Bereiding
Linzen Kikkererwten Doperwten
als alternatief voor RIJST
100% gemaakt van Peulvruchten
Glutenvrij
9 MIN. KOKEN
van nature bron van vezels en eiwitten

AH
BROODSTROOISELS

RETAILER: Albert Heijn

COUNTRY: The Netherlands

CATEGORY: G3. Packaged Goods

AGENCY: dBOD

CREDITS:

Brand Director/Strategy: Evelyn Hille / dBOD / VBAT

Group Senior Design Director: Ditte Glebbeek / dBOD / VBAT

Group Designer: Fernando Ibanez / dBOD / VBAT

Group Illustrations: Jasmijn Evans / Art Associates

CONSUM
RECETA PREMIUM

RETAILER: Consum

COUNTRY: Spain

CATEGORY: B1. New Brand

AGENCY: Supermercados Consum

CREDITS:

Account Directors - Managing Directors: Marta Álvarez / Ana Niño

Strategic Planning: Ana Niño

Creative Director: Pau Rodilla

Art Director: Jordi Escrivá

WORLD MARKET HOLIDAY

RETAILER: World Market

COUNTRY: USA

CATEGORY: B4. Holiday Or Limited-Edition

AGENCY: In house design at Cost Plus World Market

CREDITS:

Art Director: Jeffrey Pelo

Art Direction and Design: Carrie Binney

Design: Christa Compomizzo-Ruiz

Production: Mike Lippert

Photography: Steve Underwood

UNIQUELY J SPARKLING WATER

RETAILER: Jet.com
COUNTRY: USA
CATEGORY: G6. Beverages: Non-Alcoholic
AGENCY: Elmwood Design Inc.
CREDITS:
Brand Manager: Jamie Krusewicz Jet.com & Jet.com Private Brand Team
Elmwood Design Inc.
Art Director: Samantha Barbagiovanni
Designer: Connie Ahn
Illustrators: Irradie

UNIQUELY J
SNACK NUTS

RETAILER: Jet.com

COUNTRY: USA

CATEGORY: G3. Packaged Goods

AGENCY: Elmwood Design Inc.

CREDITS:

Brand Manager: Jamie Krusewicz Jet.com & Jet.com Private Brand Team

Elmwood Design Inc.

AD: Samantha Barbagiovanni

Designer: Tet Marti

Illustrator: C.M. Butzer

JUMBO VEGETABLE MILK

RETAILER: Jumbo Supermarkets

COUNTRY: The Netherlands

CATEGORY: G6. Beverages: Non-Alcoholic

AGENCY: OD designstudio

CREDITS:

Concept: OD

Design: Menno Mulder

Illustration: OD

Client / Brand Manager: Jumbo Supermarkets, Sabine Snijders-Simons

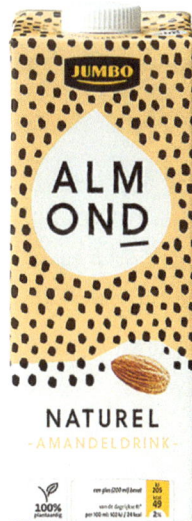

CONSUM SMOOTHIES

RETAILER: Supermercados Consum
COUNTRY: Spain
CATEGORY: G6. Beverages: Non-Alcoholic
AGENCY: Rosebud/Consum
CREDITS:
Account management: María José Alonso
Account executive: Marta Celada
Art and design management: Amparo Doménech
Creative conceptualization: Ana María Tebar

AH
FARM DAIRY

RETAILER: Albert Heijn
COUNTRY: The Netherlands
CATEGORY: G2: Organic And Natural Food
AGENCY: dBOD
CREDITS:
Brand Director / Strategy: Evelyn Hille / dBOD / VBAT Group
Senior Design Director: Ditte Glebbeek / dBOD / VBAT Group
Designer: Fernando Ibanez / dBOD / VBAT Group
Illustrations: Harald Sprenkeling / dBOD / VBAT Group

CONSUM ZUMASTÉ

RETAILER: Supermercados Consum
COUNTRY: Spain
CATEGORY: G6. Beverages: Non-Alcoholic
AGENCY: Rosebud/Consum
CREDITS:
Account management: María José Alonso
Account executive: Marta Celada
Art and design management: Amparo Doménech
Creative conceptualization: Sira Mollá

SPECIALLY SELECTED

RETAILER: Aldi
COUNTRY: Australia
CATEGORY: G3. Packaged Goods
AGENCY: Equator Design
CREDITS:
Design Director: Nick Wilson
Design Director: Glyn Robinson
Designer: Simon Kirk
Creative Account Manager: Karl Dixon
Artwork Account Manager: Martin Barnes
Artwork Account Manager: Paul McNulty
Senior Photographer: Stewart Bimson
Food Stylist: Pam Witter

SENSATIONS CLUCK-WING SAUCE

RETAILER: Sobeys
COUNTRY: Canada
CATEGORY: G3. Packaged Goods
AGENCY: Fish out of Water Design
CREDITS:
Brand Manager: Bonnie McCrone
Art Direction: Sarah Grundy
Designer: Janet New
Account Manager: Jennifer Harvey
Pre-Press: Autumn Graphics
Printer: Fort Dearborn Company

2019 VERTEX AWARDS

DERMA365 SENSITIVE SKINCARE

RETAILER: Mannings
COUNTRY: Hong Kong
CATEGORY: B1. New Brand
AGENCY: Passionfruit Asia Ltd
CREDITS:
Client lead: Antoinette Lasjunies
Project leader: Craig Briggs
Designers: Harumi Kubo, Liem Cheung
Strategy lead: Nao Design Trends

JUST GRANOLA

RETAILER: Fresh Direct

COUNTRY: USA

CATEGORY: G3. Packaged Goods

AGENCY: Daymon Creative Services

CREDITS:

Vice President, Merchandising: Carrie Mesing

HT TRADERS PIZZA

RETAILER: Harris Teeter
COUNTRY: USA
CATEGORY: G4. Frozen
AGENCY: Daymon Creative Services
CREDITS:
Agency: Harris Teeter & Daymon Creative Services
DCS Design Director: Felix Rosales
DCS Photographer: Autumn Underwood
Harris Teeter Advertising & Creative Services: Steve Kent, Kim Davis

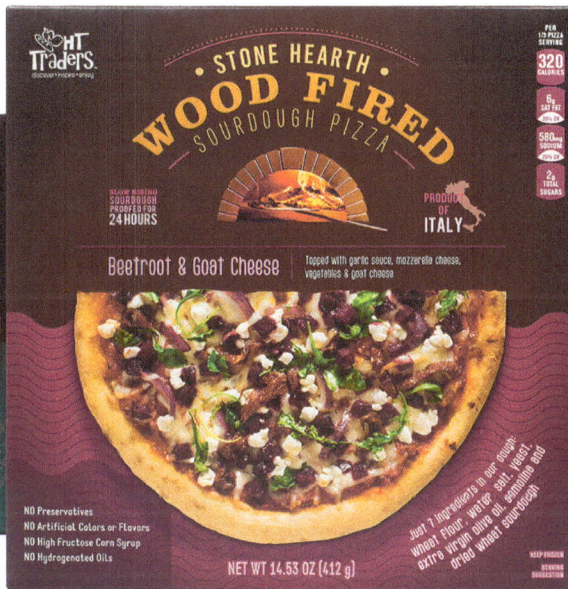

IRRESISTIBLES SHERBET

RETAILER: Metro s.e.n.c.
COUNTRY: Canada
CATEGORY: G4. Frozen
AGENCY: Pigeon Brands
CREDITS:
Director: Marie Horodecki-Ayme
Brand Manager: Éric Gagnon
Photographer: Alain Sirois Illustrator: Alain Massicotte Art
Director: Olivier Chevillot
Designer: Jessika Neal
Production Direction: Phillipe Morin
Phillipe Morin Manager: Armelle Dubourg
Printer: Stanpac
Pré-press: Stanpac

FRESH THYME CEREAL

RETAILER: Fresh Thyme Farmers Market
COUNTRY: USA
CATEGORY: G3. Packaged Goods
AGENCY: The Creative Pack
CREDITS:
Creative Director: Danielle Beal
Designer: Heather Storie
Project Manager: Fern Serna

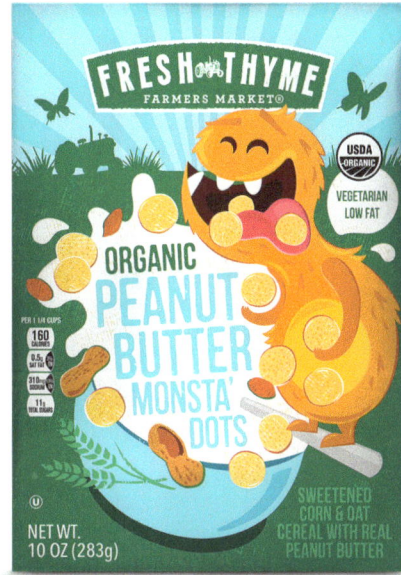

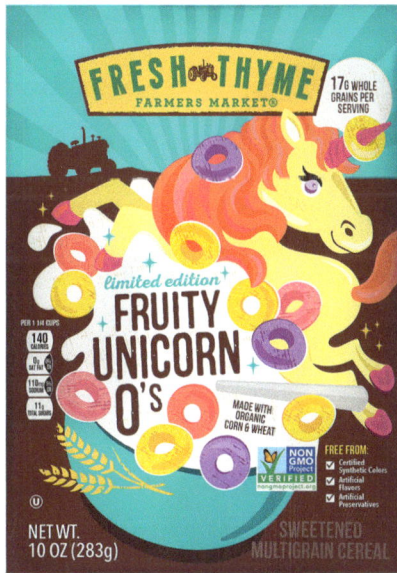

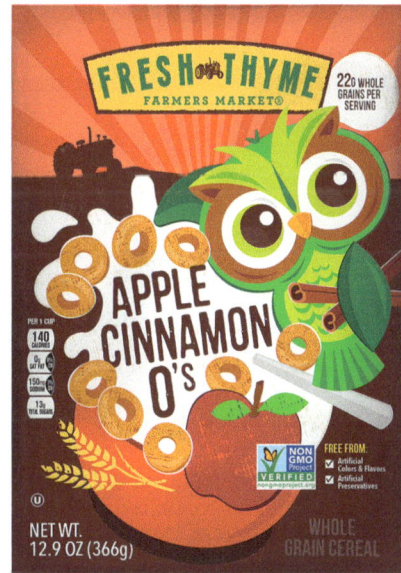

MASK ME AMORE FACE MASK

RETAILER: EUROCASH / KONTIGO
COUNTRY: POLAND
CATEGORY: B1. New Brand
AGENCY: Aleksandra Szmak STUDIO
CREDITS:
Creative Direction: Aleksandra Szmak

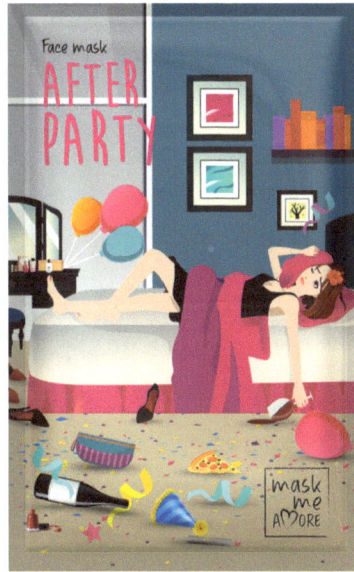

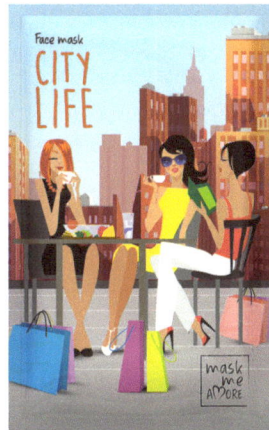

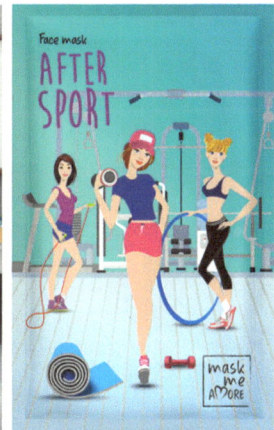

NOMA
ADVANCED

RETAILER: Canadian Tire
COUNTRY: Canada
CATEGORY: B2. Redesigned Brand
AGENCY: St. Joseph Communications Content Group
CREDITS:
Designer (SJC): John Shanks
Creative Director (SJC): Dennis Benoit
Account Director (SJC): Bryan Raymond
Brand Manager (Canadian Tire): Crystal Caughill

NOMA
ADVANCED
CONSTANT-LIT
Pure White String Lights
100
INDOOR/OUTDOOR
MINI LEDs
PURE WHITE
LED
NOMA
ADVANCED
CONSTANT-LIT
Warm White Cluster Lights
Grappe de lumières blanc chaud
TOUJOURS ALLUMÉ
150
3 MM LEDs
DEL 3 MM
WARM WHITE
BLANC CHAUD
NOMA
ADVANCED
CONSTANT-LIT
Warm White String
100
INDOOR/OUTDOOR
MINI LEDs
WARM WHITE
NOMA
ADVANCED
CONSTANT-LIT
Pure White String Lights
ADVANCED STRAND TECHNOLOGY
WEATHER SEALED SOCKETS
YEAR LIMITED WARRANTY
LENGTH
33' 7"
BULBS
C9
TOTAL WATTAGE
6
PURE WHITE
LED
50
INDOOR/OUTDOOR
C9 LEDs

PRINCE & SPRING LYT WATER

RETAILER: Boxed.com

COUNTRY: USA

CATEGORY: G6. Beverages: Non-Alcoholic

AGENCY: Boxed

CREDITS:

VP Private Brands: Jeff Gamsey

Creative Director: Chris Cheung

VP Design: Ryan Carl

Senior Product Developer: Brandon Wehmeyer

Package Designer: Monica Kim

Brand Manager: Annslee Deluca

Photography: Maged Samuel, Marissa Rosado & Katie Dunphy

EL CORTE INGLÉS FRESH SAUCES

RETAILER: El Corte Inglés
COUNTRY: Spain
CATEGORY: G1. Fresh
AGENCY: Supperstudio
CREDITS:
Creative Director: Paco Adín
Account Director: Lourdes Morillas
Account Manager: Susana Seijas
El Corte Inglés Corporate Private Label Brand Management: José A. Rojano

PRINCE & SPRING STELLAR SELTZER

RETAILER: Boxed.com
COUNTRY: USA
CATEGORY: G6. Beverages: Non-Alcoholic
AGENCY: Boxed
CREDITS:
VP Private Brands: Jeff Gamsey
Creative Director: Chris Cheung
VP Design: Ryan Carl
Package Designer: Monica Kim
Brand Manager: Annslee Deluca

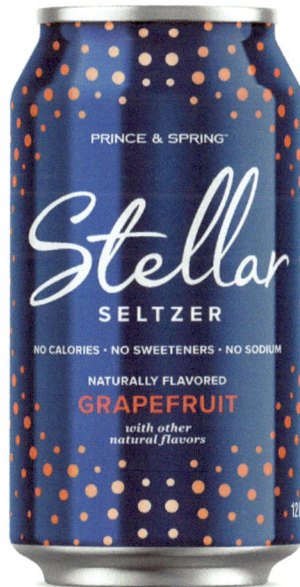

GROFERS

RETAILER: Grofers
COUNTRY: India
CATEGORY: G3. Packaged Goods
AGENCY: Yellow Dress Retail
CREDITS:
Creative Director: Michelle Romeo-Wiegman
Designer: Quino van Schaik

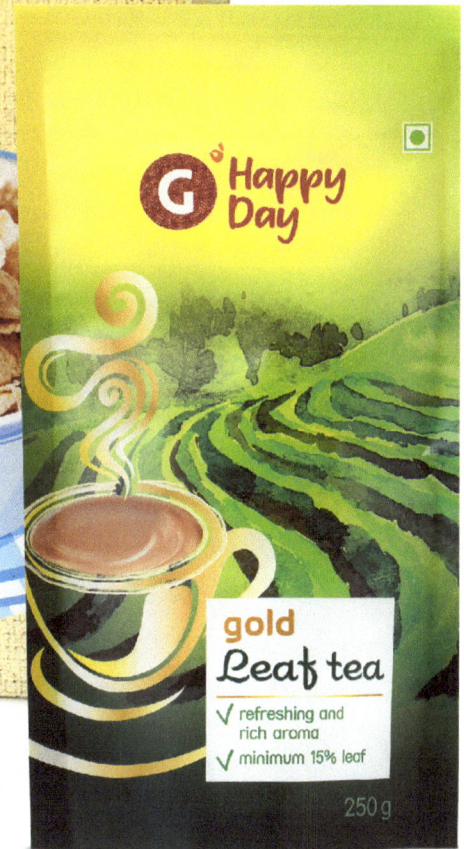

EL CORTE INGLÉS
BOOM·BALLS

RETAILER: El Corte Inglés

COUNTRY: Spain

CATEGORY: G3. Packaged Goods

AGENCY: Supperstudio

CREDITS:

Creative Director: Paco Adín

Account Director: Lourdes Morillas

Account Manager: Susana Seijas

El Corte Inglés Corporate Private Label Brand Management: José A. Rojano

Boom
balls
Bolas de maíz con miel
Bolas de milho com mel
Corn balls with honey
Boom
balls
Bolas de maíz con cacao
Bolas de milho com cacau
Corn balls with cocoa

EL CORTE INGLÉS FILLED CEREALS

RETAILER: El Corte Inglés
COUNTRY: Spain
CATEGORY: G3. Packaged Goods
AGENCY: Supperstudio
CREDITS:
Creative Director: Paco Adín
Account Director: Lourdes Morillas
Susana Seijas. Account Manager
El Corte Inglés Corporate Private Label Brand Management: José A. Rojano

Milk
&Cream
Almohadillas rellenas
de crema con leche
Amofainhas recheas
de creme com leite
Pillows filled with a milky cream
FUENTE DE FIBRA
CON 8 VITAMINAS
& HIERRO
500g

Choco
&Cream
Almohadillas rellenas de crema
de chocolate con avellanas
Amofainhas recheas de creme
com chocolate e aveãs
Pillows filled with a cream
with chocolate and hazelnuts
FUENTE DE FIBRA
CON 8 VITAMINAS
& HIERRO
500g

FRED'S CANNED FRUIT & VEG

RETAILER: Fred's Inc.
COUNTRY: USA
CATEGORY: G3. Packaged Goods
AGENCY: Marketing By Design
CREDITS:
Creative Director & Designer: David Ziegler-Voll
Production Artist: Deanna Vosburgh
Project Manager: Ashley Smits
Account Manager: Christopher Thaemert

PADDY CAKES

RETAILER: Fred's Inc.
COUNTRY: USA
CATEGORY: P7. Baby
AGENCY: Marketing By Design
CREDITS:
Creative Director & Designer: David Ziegler-Voll
Production Artist: Deanna Vosburgh
Project Manager: Ashley Smits
Account Manager: Christopher Thaemert

TASTE OF INSPIRATIONS

RETAILER: Ahold Delhaize
COUNTRY: USA
CATEGORY: B1. New Brand
AGENCY: Ahold Delhaize Private Brands
CREDITS:
SVP of Private Brands: Juan DePaoli
Private Brands Director: Tesha Sigmon
Design Manager: Marygrace Bianco
Designer: Tommy Tran
Designer: Cameron Parson

WORLD MARKET PASTA SAUCE

RETAILER: Cost Plus World Market

COUNTRY: USA

CATEGORY: G3. Packaged Goods

AGENCY: created in house at Cost Plus World Market

CREDITS:

Jeffrey Pelo and Carrie Binney, Art Direction and Design

Jeffrey Pelo, Hand Lettering

Mike Lippert, Production

Steve Underwood, Photography

STARBUCKS CHIPS

RETAILER: Starbucks
COUNTRY: Spain / Portugal
CATEGORY: G3. Packaged Goods
AGENCY: Supperstudio
CREDITS:
Creative Director: Paco Adin
Account Director: Lourdes Morillas

BRO

2019 VERTEX AWARDS

NZE

WUMART SNACKS

RETAILER: Wumart
COUNTRY: China
CATEGORY: G2: Organic And Natural Food
AGENCY: Dmall Life
CREDITS:
Brand Manager: Jing Huang
Creative Director: Jing Xu
Designer: Xiao Fang Lin, Meng Jia Wang
Photographer: Xin Yu Zhao
Writer: Joan Liang, Chungxing Mah

M INSTANT SOUP

RETAILER: Makro
COUNTRY: South Africa
CATEGORY: G3. Packaged Goods
AGENCY: Daymon Worldwide
CREDITS:
Brand Manager: Stacey Read
Photographer: Celeste Betz
Designer: Celeste Betz

JUST FROZEN FRUIT

RETAILER: Fresh Direct

COUNTRY: USA

CATEGORY: G4. Frozen

AGENCY: Daymon Creative Services

CREDITS:

Vice President, Merchandising: Carrie Mesing

HT TRADERS GELATO

RETAILER: Harris Teeter
COUNTRY: USA
CATEGORY: G4. Frozen
AGENCY: Daymon Creative Services
CREDITS:
Daymon Design Director: Felix Rosales
Harris Teeter Advertising & Creative Services: Steve Kent/Kim Davis

WEGMANS PICKLES

RETAILER: Wegmans
COUNTRY: USA
CATEGORY: G3. Packaged Goods
AGENCY: Wallace Church & Co.
CREDITS:
Wegmans Marketing Team: Jaime Torres
Executive Creative Director: Stan Church
Creative Director: John Bruno
Associate Creative Director: Jodi Lubrich
Designer: Diana Luistro
Account Manager: Maureen McKenna

IRRESISTIBLES EGGNOG

RETAILER: Metro s.e.n.c.
COUNTRY: Canada
CATEGORY: G6. Beverages: Non-Alcoholic
AGENCY: Pigeon Brands
CREDITS:
Brand manager: Marie Horodecki-Aymes / Éric Gagnon
Photography: David DeStefano
Illustration: Jessie Ford
Art Director: Olivier Chevillot
Designer: Jessika Neal
Production direction: Phillipe Morin
Manager: Armelle Dubourg
Printer: Elopak
Pré-presse: Elopak

DISCOUNT WITH A PURPOSE

RETAILER: REMA 1000
COUNTRY: Denmark
CATEGORY: B2. Redesigned Brand
AGENCY: Everland
CREDITS:
Design Lead: Pernille Dueholm
Client Director: Ronnie Erik Greve
Senior Project Manager: Kenneth Egeland Schou
Strategy Director: Christian Halsted

BEM ME QUER

RETAILER: Modelo Continente Hipermercados SA
COUNTRY: Portugal
CATEGORY: B4. Holiday Or Limited-Edition
AGENCY: Sonae MC Packaging & Design Team
CREDITS:
Sonae MC Packaging & Design Team
Designer: Inês Brito

SIGNATURE
SELECT ASIAN

RETAILER: Albertsons

COUNTRY: USA

CATEGORY: G8. International/Specialty Food

AGENCY: Trinity Brand Group

CREDITS:

Creative Director: Paul Kagiwada

Designers: Dexter Lee, Quentin Bangston

Strategy Director: Laurie Kreisberg

Client Manager: Kyle Showen

Product Manager: Eugene Buczynski

EARTH FARE ORGANIC

RETAILER: Earth Fare
COUNTRY: USA
CATEGORY: B1. New Brand
AGENCY: SailPointe Creative
CREDITS:
Vice President of Brand Management: Jen Linke
Client Services Director: Kevin Keene
Art Director: Robert Rios
Senior Designer: Ellen Freedman
Design Team: Susan McGarrity, Heather Deiber
Lead Account Manager: Lynne Traci
Photographer: Doug Human
Production Manager: Jeff Camp

JUMBO COOKIES

RETAILER: Jumbo supermarkten B.V.
COUNTRY: The Netherlands
CATEGORY: G3. Packaged Goods
AGENCY: Guts&Glorious
CREDITS:
Jumbo Supermarkets
Private Label Manager: Iris van den Berg
Assortiments Manager: Linda Schellekens
Guts&Glorious
Creative Direction/Design: Heidi Boersma, Vincent Limburg
Illustration: Willemijn de Lint
Koekenbakkerij Veldt: Harold Gierman

TINY TALES

RETAILER: PetSmart
COUNTRY: USA
CATEGORY: G7. Pet Products
AGENCY: PetSmart
CREDITS:
Director of Proprietary Brand Design: Amy Rhodes
Art Director: Paul Henson
Senior Copywriter: Kristin Frank
Product Designers: Jeff Watson and Paul Tamulewicz
Illustrator: Dean MacAdam
Photographer: Jason Pease
Director, Proprietary Brands: Brian Quinn

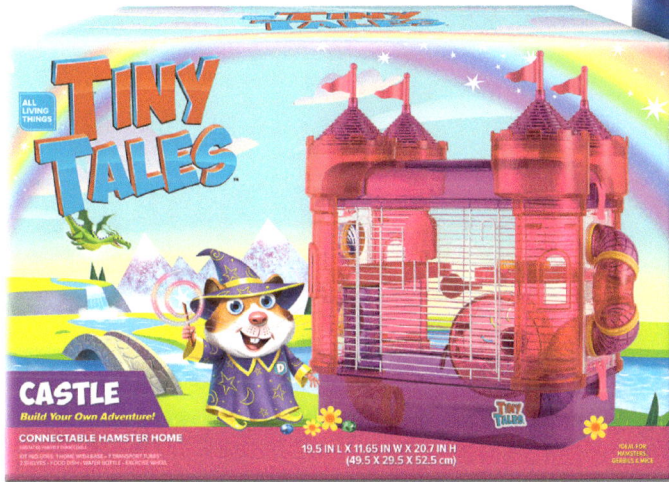

CASTLE

Build Your Own Adventure!

CONNECTABLE HAMSTER HOME

19.5 IN L X 11.65 IN W X 20.7 IN H
(49.5 X 29.5 X 52.5 cm)

ROCKET SHIP

Build Your Own Adventure!

CONNECTABLE HAMSTER HOME

IN DIA X 24.6 IN H (40 X 62.4 cm)

LIGHTS UP!

OFFICE DEPOT HOLIDAY PAPER

RETAILER: Office Depot Office Max
COUNTRY: USA
CATEGORY: B4. Holiday Or Limited-Edition
AGENCY: Office Depot
CREDITS:
Brand Managers: Rachel Tibor, Josie Sandoval
Creative Lead: Danielle Stella-Fischer
Design Manager: Marjolijn Elbert-Chung
Graphic Designer: Karla Butler
Production Designer: Maximus Kahng
Print Manager: Sharon Gross

ACTION THE ENERGY DRINK

RETAILER: ACTION
COUNTRY: Netherlands
CATEGORY: G6. Beverages: Non-Alcoholic
AGENCY: Yellow Dress Retail
CREDITS:
Brand Manager: Erwin Wentink
Creative Director: Michelle Romeo-Wiegman
Designer: Tamas Paszto
Illustrator: Willemijn de Lint

SCHNUCKS SNACKING NUTS

RETAILER: Schnucks
COUNTRY: USA
CATEGORY: G3. Packaged Goods
AGENCY: Equator Design
CREDITS:
Creative Director: Jennifer Gaeto
Lead Designer: Don Dzielinski
Photographer: Stewart Bimson
Account Director: Alyssa Cioffi

7-SELECT POOFY PUFFS

RETAILER: 7-Eleven
COUNTRY: USA
CATEGORY: G3. Packaged Goods
AGENCY: Marketing By Design
CREDITS:
Creative Director: David Ziegler-Voll
Production Artist: Deanna Vosburgh
Illustration: David Ziegler-Voll
Photographer: Jim Scherer
Account Manager: Austin Sniezek

NATURAL GROCERS BEEF JERKY

RETAILER: Natural Grocers
COUNTRY: USA
CATEGORY: G3. Packaged Goods
AGENCY: Marketing By Design
CREDITS:
Art Director: Sandra Button
Designer: Becca Marko
Production Artist: Angie Beighle & Dan Cosco
Project Manager: Ivana Baric

FAIRWAY ORGANIC GRAINS

RETAILER: Fairway Market
COUNTRY: USA
CATEGORY: G2: Organic And Natural Food
AGENCY: Nancy Frame Design, LLC
CREDITS:
Brand manager: Jason Bidart, Fairway Market
Package design: Nancy Frame
Photographer: Bob Frame

WOOLWORTHS MUESLI

RETAILER: Woolworths
COUNTRY: Australia
CATEGORY: G3. Packaged Goods
AGENCY: Marque Brand Consultants
CREDITS:
Design Director: Wendy Laws
Account Director: Nicola Richards
Brand Manager: Kate Walker
Design Specialist: Alice Johnson

ETOS MINI BATH BOMBS

RETAILER: Ahold Delhaize
COUNTRY: USA
CATEGORY: P6. Beauty
AGENCY: Ahold Delhaize Private Brands
CREDITS:
Senior Vice President, Own Brands: Juan De Paoli
Private Brands Director: Kasey Sheffer
Creative Director: Paul Skozilas
Art Director, Designer: April Snider

PRICE RITE

RETAILER: Price Rite
COUNTRY: USA
CATEGORY: G3. Packaged Goods
AGENCY: CBX

WAWA COLD BREW COFFEE

RETAILER: Wawa
COUNTRY: USA
CATEGORY: G6. Beverages: Non-Alcoholic
AGENCY: CBX

CO-OP
CHRISTMAS

RETAILER: CO-OP

COUNTRY: UK

CATEGORY: B4. Holiday Or Limited-Edition

AGENCY: Equator Design

CREDITS:

Brand Manager: Brooke Fletcher, Caron Moore

Account Manager: Sally Hunter

Art director/Designer: Heather Armer

Photography: Tom Law, Emma Prothero

Food and prop stylists: Pam Witter, Dawn Wormald

UNIQUELY J
GREEN PAPER

RETAILER: Jet.com

COUNTRY: USA

CATEGORY: H2. Home Care: paper products, trash bags, batteries, light bulbs, etc.

AGENCY: Elmwood Design Inc.

CREDITS:

Brand Manager: Jamie Krusewicz Jet.com & Jet.com Private Brand Team

Elmwood Design Inc.

Art Director: Samantha Barbagiovanni

Designer: Samantha Barbagiovanni

Illustrator: May Van Milligen

friends
of forests

paper
towels
huge
6 rolls

GES

JUDGES

PACO ADIN
Creative Director
Supperstudio
Spain

RICK BARRACK
Chief Creative Officer & Managing Partner
CBX
New York, USA

DANIELLE BEAL
Creative Director
The Creative Pack
California, USA

PAULA BUNNY
Creative Director, Brother Design
Brother Design
New Zealand

CONNIE CAO
Senior Graphic Designer
ACE Global Distribution (Shanghai) Ltd. a subsidiary of ACE Hardware Corporation USA
China

CHRIS CHEUNG
Co-founder
Boxed
New York, USA

CHARLENE CODNER
Founder & Chief Creative Officer
Fish out of Water Design
Ontario, Canada

STEVEN COX
Creative Director
Daymon
Connecticut, USA

MARIA DUBUC

President, MBD
Vice President, Big Red Rooster
Marketing by Design (MBD)
Massachusetts, USA

MICHAEL DUFFY

Group Creative Director & Partner
Equator Design
Illinois, USA

GUILLERMO DUFRANC

Private Brand Design Director
TridImage
Argentina

MASANORI ETO

Creative Director
AdBrain, Inc.
Tokyo, Japan

LOE LIMPENS

Managing Partner
Yellow Dress Retail
Amsterdam, Netherlands

FRED RICHARDS

CCO & Partner
Kaleidoscope
Chicago, USA

JENS SIEVERT

Creative Director
Daymon International
Lisbon, Portugal

NICK VAUS

Partner & Creative Director
Free the Birds
United Kingdom

ZHOU WENJUN

Founder, Creative Director & Architect
524 Studio
China

CHRISTOPHER DURHAM

Co-founder, the Vertex Awards
President, My Private Brand
Charlotte, NC

MY [PRIVATE] BRAND

My Private Brand was launched by Christopher Durham in late 2008 and has quickly become the most widely read daily publication on Private Brands in the world. It's the leading resource for retailer owned Brand development, analysis, best practices, news, information and jobs. With readership from retailers, private brand manufacturers, branding agencies and thought leaders from around the world, My Private Brand is designed to foster innovation, encourage debate and write the next chapter of brand management— Private Brand Management.

Christopher Durham is a world-renowned private brand consultant, author, and retailer who built million-dollar brands for global supermarket retailer Delhaize and led strategy and brand development for Lowe's Home Improvement's $18 billion private brand portfolio. He is the founder of the groundbreaking private brand website My Private Brand and the co-founder of the international private brand package design competition The Vertex Awards. In 2017 he introduced Velocity: The My Private Brand Conference a thought leadership gathering of private brand executives focused on creating the future or retail owned brands.

He has consulted with retailers around the world on their private brand portfolios including Ahold, Family Dollar, Petco, Staples, Office Depot, Best Buy, Metro (Canada), TLW (Taiwan) REI and Hola (Taiwan).

Durham has published six definitive books on private brands, including his first book, Fifty2: The My Private Brand Project and his newest book, Vanguard: Vintage Originals, a visual tour of innovation, disruption and design in private brand dating back to the mid-1800's.

Dynamic in his presentation while down to earth and frank in his opinions, he has presented at numerous conferences, including FUSE, The Dieline Conference, Packaging that Sells, Omnishopper and PLMA'a annual trade show in Chicago and Amsterdam.

PHILLIP RUSSO

Co-founder, the Vertex Awards
Founder/Publisher/Editor, Global Retail Brands
New York, NY

Global Retail Brands

Global Retail Brands magazine was launched to promote the best examples of retail brand marketing from around the world. Industry experts from all facets of private label contribute to the magazine, providing an unbiased, international voice of authority. Its design departs from the norm to reflect the industry's creativity.

Phillip is the Founder/Publisher/Editor of Global Retail Brands magazine and a 18-year veteran of the private label industry. He was responsible for Private Label magazine's global expansion and return to profitability prior to the successful launch of Global Retail Brands.

His appreciation for design and its successful application is rooted in the design field, where he headed a trade publishing division which produced trade shows, magazines and digital for the commercial interior design industry. Before Private Label, he was publisher of the modern design/lifestyle magazine, DWELL, one of the most successful magazine launches of its time.

He is the principal of Kent Media, based in New York City, which publishes Global Retail Brands and a number of Design Show directories.

THANK YOU

TO OUR SPONSORS WHO GRACIOUSLY SUPPORT THE VERTEX AWARDS

MBD

MBDESIGN.COM

coloredge®

COLOREDGE.COM

teri

TERISTUDIOS.COM

VOCCÏİ

VOCCII.COM